D1305060

GUIDED by HIS LIGHT

A Child's Bedtime Prayer Book

GUIDED *by* HIS LIGHT

A Child's Bedtime Prayer Book

Written by
Susan Jones

Illustrated by
Pauline Siewert

Good Books

New York, New York

GOD FORGIVES MY MISTAKES

None of us are perfect.
We all make some mistakes.
But every day we're trying
to be good for Jesus' sake.

God forgives our messes
when we ask Him to.
He loves us all the time,
no matter what we do.

God Protects Me

I snuggle in and close my eyes,
then I start counting sheep.
Soon starry dreams and happy things
will come my way in sleep.

God is watching over me
with tenderness and might.
He guards me with an endless love
and keeps me safe all night.

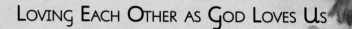

Loving Each Other as God Loves Us

My best friend means a lot to me;
he makes each moment fun.
I know that I can count on him
just like the rising sun.

And just the same I'm there for him
to help him reach new heights.
One special gift that I can give
is friendship warm and bright.

God's Words Bring Comfort

"Do not be afraid," God says,
"I am there wherever you go."
His words are like the softest hug
when I am feeling low.

As cozy as a blanket,
surrounding me like fleece,
the words the Lord has spoken
bring me comfort, warmth, and peace.

GOD MADE EVERYTHING

Every creature here on land
is made by God with His own hand:
the dappled deer, the buzzing bee,
and people just like you and me.

Whether you have skin or fur,
or if you laugh or bark or purr,
you're lovely 'cause you're God's design.
You're special 'cause God says, "You're mine!"

GOD IS BEAUTIFUL

I caught a glimpse of God today:
He sparkled and He glowed.
His miracles are everywhere;
I see them and I know.

I caught a glimpse of God today,
so beautiful a sight.
I'll catch it to remind me
of God's love shining bright.

I Send God My Prayers

Dear God, I have a message
I know you'll want to hear.
I'll whisper you this prayer
'cause I know that you are near.

Thank you for my family
and this bright, shining day.
It feels so good to tell you:
I feel blessed in every way.

Faith Is Blooming in Me

My mother plants a little seed,
and, like my faith, it grows.
It flowers when the season's right;
its colors start to show.

Each day I learn about my faith,
I listen and I pray,
and as it blooms I hope that I
can share it too one day.

I'm Guided by God's Light

The full moon glows above me
and blankets me in light.
It's time to tell the Lord above
what I'm grateful for tonight.

Thank you Lord, for blessing me,
my heart is full of love.
You give me hope and strength and care,
and guidance from above.

FAMILY IS A TREASURE

Family is a golden gift;
it's precious and it's true.
Jesus says to honor them
in everything you do.

When we're together, it feels just right.
I love my family with all my might.

Jesus Teaches Kindness

Jesus tells us: Shine your light,
be kind without a doubt.
I'm small but I can do big things,
like helping people out.

When someone needs me I'll be sure
to do all I can do.
It makes me glad to know that I
can be like Jesus too.

God Is Always by My Side

God is in the mama bear
who guards her newborn cub.
He's there when my mom comforts me
with reassuring hugs.
A puppy's kiss upon my cheek
feels heaven-sent to me.
These signs of love remind me
just how caring God can be.
Wherever I go, whatever I do,
I'll never feel alone.
I'll feel God's love around me
wherever I may roam.

I Can Help My Family

Mom likes it when I help her out;
I see it in her eyes.
She sees that I can do a lot
despite my smaller size.

Every time I help her,
she gives my head a pat,
and then I know she's proud of me,
and I'm so glad for that.

GOD IS EVERYWHERE

God is in the beautiful doves
that soar up in the skies above.
He's in the fish that swim so fast
between the waves in oceans vast.
He's blowing in the gentle breeze.
He's everywhere; a sign of peace.

A Song of Praise

I've gathered all the members
of my closest family.
Today I'd like to sing God's praise
in perfect harmony.

Your love is like a melody
that makes my spirit soar;
my heart's an open songbook:
each day I love you more.

GOD GIVES ME STRENGTH

When I'm tired from a very long day,
and my strength is nearly gone,
I know that God will carry me
through darkness into dawn.

His love will raise me up so high,
and then He'll light my way,
just as a rainbow gives me hope
after a stormy day.

GOD MADE ME SPECIAL

Each newborn creature is unique
before it starts to hatch,
and I have something special
that no one else can match.

God blessed me with a special spark;
it shines with His own light.
I'm lovely just the way I am,
'cause God made me just right.

GOD IS IN THE STILLNESS

There's nothing like a quiet space
to help me think and pray.
In silent moments I enjoy
some time with God each day.

When all is hushed and peaceful;
when all is still and calm,
I notice God is there with me,
just like my favorite Psalm.

My soul is joyful in the Lord,
His presence feels so near.
In quiet times I'm close with God;
His voice is soft and clear.

GOD LISTENS WHEN I'M SAD

God listens close to what I say,
even though I'm small.
He bends down low to hear me
when I cry, or when I fall.

With a smile, He says to me:
"Don't worry. Speak up, dear.
Let your troubles be heard by me,
for I am always near."

I wipe my tears and dry my eyes,
and soon my pain is gone.
It's good to know God hears my cries;
it helps me to move on.

I Count My Blessings

I look around and all I see
are the wonderful things you've given me.
I'm lucky, God, that I am blessed
with family, friends, and all the rest.

My house, my pets whom I adore,
the toys I play with on the floor—
when I take stock of all this stuff,
I know I can't thank you enough.

Angels Are God's Messengers

Angels are such marvelous things,
with glowing halo and mighty wings.
They're messengers from up above;
they share God's grace and send His love.

They flutter through our darkest days;
sometimes they're in disguise.
Angels are our friends on Earth:
God's heavenly surprise.

My Heart Is Full of Joy

Every day brings all new blessings,
and joyful moments too,
like teddy bears and puppy love
and wagon rides for two.

Each moment fills my happy heart—
like a cup it overflows.
How God can give me so much joy
I'll never, ever know.

I'm Still Growing and Learning

Mom says kids should make mistakes,
it's how they learn and grow,
but I wish my successes
were the only acts you'd know.

Forgive me, God, I'm only young,
I try my best each day.
Please teach me how to follow you
and live my life your way.

God's Love Is Perfect

I picked a perfect seashell
while walking on the sand.
The sun was shining warmly
at your heavenly command.

I raised it up to show you;
I knew you were above.
This seashell was a symbol
of your perfect kind of love.

God Gives Us Family

When Gram and Papa visit me,
we like to sit and share
our favorite books and stories
to show how much we care.

Dad says that God is there with us
when love brings us together.
These acts of kindness teach us how
to understand God better.

Praise God!

Come on, let's all join in and sing
about the love that Jesus brings.
He shows us how to live our lives,
and teaches us to do what's right.

You play your drum, I'll twirl around:
we'll make a celebration sound!
I'll clap my hands and sing a song,
"I'll love you, God, my whole life long!"

I Follow the Golden Rule

God teaches us to do to others
as we'd want done to us,
so when someone nearby is sad,
I do what's kind and just.

It's nice to do the right thing,
and God helps me to see
that when it's my turn to be sad,
my friend is there for me.

I Am Grateful

Thank you for my daily bread,
I'll never want too much.
I wait for it so patiently—
in your good gifts I trust.

We say Grace and sit down to eat,
we're blessed to have this food.
I'd never just bite into it
because I know that's rude.

There are so many tempting things
that I might want to take.
Instead I'll follow God's good word,
and gladly I will wait.

I Say My Prayers

I say my prayers every night
and name the ones I love,
whether they are here
or safe with God above.

God bless Grandpa and Auntie, too,
and cousins far and wide.
Each one of them is part of me,
they're always by my side.

I like to think they bless me too
while lying in their beds.
Family is the greatest thing,
just like my daddy says.

God Loves Me as I Am

At school I do what I am told,
at church I sit and pray,
at home I help my mother out,
and let her guide my way.

But when the chores have all been done
and I can go outside,
I dangle from the monkey bars
and show my silly side.

I'm thankful that I'm just a kid,
it's good to have some fun.
I have to get my wiggles out,
and skip and jump and run.

God knows this and He loves me,
I'm filled with His good grace,
and when He looks upon me,
there's a smile on His face.

Susan Jones is a mother, Sunday school teacher, and writer. She lives with her family and two dogs in Manchester-by-the-Sea, Massachusetts.

Pauline Siewert spent her early childhood in East Africa before finally settling in the UK. She went to art schools in Wimbledon and Kingston, studying graphic design and illustration. She enjoys illustrating children's books from a garden studio in Farnham where she lives with her husband and a succession of rescued tortoiseshell cats.

Good Books books may be purchased in bulk at special discounts for sales promotion, corporate gifts, fund-raising, or educational purposes. Special editions can also be created to specifications. For details, contact the Special Sales Department, Good Books, 307 West 36th Street, 11th Floor, New York, NY 10018 or info@skyhorsepublishing.com.

Good Books is an imprint of Skyhorse Publishing, Inc.®, a Delaware corporation.

Visit our website at www.goodbooks.com.

10 9 8 7 6 5 4 3 2 1

Library of Congress Cataloging-in-Publication Data is available on file.

Print ISBN: 978-1-68099-282-3
Ebook ISBN: 978-1-68099-290-8

Cover design by Michele Trombley
Cover illustration by Pauline Siewert

Printed in China